The Green Library
A Comprehensive Guide to Sustainable Literature

Table of Contents

Chapter 1. Introduction

Unearth the future of literacy with our Special Report: "The Green Library: A Comprehensive Guide to Sustainable Literature". This enlightening report will spark your curiosity, promote learning, and inspire actions that contribute positively to our environment. Join us on a journey of discovery as we navigate the verdant world of green literature – from eco-friendly printing practices and sustainable book materials to authors championing environmental causes, and novels that speak to our planetary consciousness. Let's turn the pages together and submerge ourselves in literature that doesn't just transport us to different worlds, but also teaches us how to better cherish ours. You'll come away with a fresh understanding of how reading can be a gesture of love towards our planet – a thrilling prospect for both book-lovers and environmentalists alike. This Special Report is a must-have for those eager to enrich their minds while reducing their carbon footprints. Who knew we could revolutionize our reading habits this way? Discover the joy of becoming a sustainable reader today!

Chapter 2. The Concept of The Green Library

To lay a solid foundation for our exploration, it is imperative to understand what exactly "The Green Library" concept entails, its principles and implications, as well as the motivations behind its adoption.

The Green Library, also known as an eco-friendly library, fundamentally embodies the principle of sustainability in its operation, infrastructure, and services. It takes into account the current and future environmental impacts resulting from library practices, then shapes policies, procedures, and activities to minimize those impacts, thereby making the library a promoter and model of sustainability.

2.1. The Emergence of Green Libraries

With the increasing awareness of human impacts upon the environment, the green movement gained momentum in various societal sectors during the mid-to-late 20th century. Libraries joined this movement, recognizing their potential to affect substantial change due to their role as community hubs and educational institutions.

Early efforts focused on energy-efficient building construction and maintenance, promoting recycling programs, and using sustainable material alternatives. With time, these initiatives expanded to include Green Library management policies, green procurement, environmental literacy programs, and other sustainability practices, becoming the foundation of the Green Library concept.

2.2. Principles of Green Libraries

In the framework of a Green Library, there are certain principles that guide the entire process, which are:

1. **Environmental Responsibility** - Recognizing and actively addressing the environmental impacts of library operations.

2. **Sustainability Education** - Utilizing the library's educational platform to foster environmental literacy and inspire eco-friendly behavior amongst the library users.

3. **Energy and Resource Efficiency** - Creating a library infrastructure that focuses on minimizing the consumption of resources, utilizing renewable energy, and maximizing the use of efficient technologies.

4. **Health and Well-being** - Improving the quality of indoor environments by utilizing non-toxic materials, improving air quality, and providing natural light and spaces within the library that encourage human-nature interaction.

5. **Community Involvement** - Collaborating with local communities to encourage participation in green practices and programs.

2.3. The Green Library Infrastructure

A significant aspect of the Green Library is its physical infrastructure. To be genuinely eco-friendly, a library's construction, maintenance, and operational processes aim for minimal environmental disruption.

This could involve using renewable materials in construction, harnessing solar or wind power for energy needs, incorporating natural light optimally, and creating spaces in tune with nature. For existing libraries, retrofitting may be followed to meet green standards, such as swapping traditional lighting for LED lights, installing high-efficiency HVAC systems, or implementing water conservation measures.

2.4. Green Library Practices

Green Libraries extend the sustainability principle to daily operations and events. Initiatives may include:

- Waste Management: Implementing robust recycling programs for paper, plastics and other recyclables generated in the library.

- Procurement Policies: Purchasing products made from recycled or sustainable materials, and partnering with suppliers who adhere to green practices.

- Digital Transition: Transitioning to digital resources to save paper and energy.

- Environmental Activities: Organizing environmental education programs, cleanup drives, workshops on upcycling, and other engaging events that inspire users to embrace an eco-conscious lifestyle.

2.5. Green Library and Literature

In the context of literature, Green Libraries play a crucial role in advancing sustainable literature to users. They are repositories and propagators of eco-themes books, green authors, and environmental research. By incorporating environmental literature in their collections and promoting these books through tailored programs, Green Libraries foster a deeper understanding and appreciation amongst readers for the environment and the need for its protection.

In conclusion, The Green Library isn't just a building or a repository of books; it's an initiative, a commitment to live and promote a sustainable lifestyle. It cradles the responsibility of educating individuals about environmental impacts and driving the community towards positive sustainable practices. More importantly, it exemplifies how literature, books, their curation, and dissemination can play a crucial role in achieving environmental sustainability. Through Green Libraries, we can profoundly transform our reading habits to become a catalyst for love and care towards our planet.

Chapter 3. A Deep Dive into Sustainable Printing Practices

The seismic shift toward eco-friendly practices is not just an environmental necessity but also a business imperative. Talk of sustainable printing is no longer reserved for a small niche of eco-pioneers. Major industry players, publishing houses, authors, and readers alike are exploring ways to lessen their environmental impact. To understand how we can revolutionize our printing habits, we must first delve deep into the world of sustainable printing practices.

3.1. The Basics of Paper and Its Environmental Impact

Paper production, including pulp and paper mills, is the third largest industrial emitter of global warming gases. Additionally, the process often uses chlorine-based bleaches for whitening, which results in harmful toxins being released into the environment. This toxic waste affects both the atmosphere and bodies of water, harming wildlife and disturbing ecosystems.

Sustainable printing, therefore, seeks to mitigate these impacts by using recycled or sustainably sourced paper, alternative inks, and energy-efficient methods. Ultimately, the goal is to limit carbon emissions, energy consumption, and waste, while also fostering economic growth and social responsibility.

3.2. The Wonders of Recycled Paper

The first step toward sustainable printing is the choice of paper. Recycled paper uses less energy, water, and produces less air pollution than the paper from virgin pulp. It also limits the number of trees are cut down each year for paper production - a single ton of recycled paper saves approximately 17 trees.

Some may argue that the quality of recycled paper isn't on par with virgin paper, but the advancements in technology have improved its look and feel. You will be hard-pressed to notice a significant difference.

3.3. Unbleached and Processed Chlorine Free Paper

Beyond the recycled and virgin paper dichotomy lies an additional consideration: the bleaching process. Traditional paper production uses chlorine gas, resulting in harmful byproducts that end up in our waters.

Unbleached paper keeps its natural brown color, hence it eliminates the need for harmful bleaching agents. However, if a whiter paper is needed, there are safer alternatives to the traditional chlorine gas bleaching. Processed Chlorine-Free (PCF) paper is made from recycled fibers that haven't been re-bleached with chlorine containing compounds. Totally Chlorine Free (TCF), on the other hand, is made from virgin fibers that have been unbleached or processed with a chlorine alternative.

3.4. Introducing Alternative Inks

Sustainable printing doesn't stop at paper. The ink used for printing is another crucial component. Conventional petroleum-based inks emit Volatile Organic Compounds (VOCs) that contribute to global warming.

On a quest for sustainability, alternative inks have been developed. Soy-based inks, for instance, are widely used due to their lower VOC content. They are also significantly easier to de-ink during the recycling process. Other environmentally friendly options include water-based inks and vegetable-based inks.

3.5. Efficient Use of Resources

To further improve sustainability, printing companies are looking to optimize their use of resources. This includes reducing waste in the production process, improving energy efficiency of printing machinery, and printing on-demand to avoid overproduction.

Energy efficiency can be improved by regularly maintaining equipment to ensure it runs optimally, employing power saving techniques, and sourcing energy from renewable energy sources. Overproduction can be avoided by using data to predict demand and print accordingly. Sustainability should encompass all stages of the printing process, from design to delivery.

3.6. The Role of Certifications

To ensure sustainable practices, various certification schemes have been established. These certifications help customers recognize companies prioritizing environmental responsibility.

The Forest Stewardship Council (FSC) certification, for instance, signifies that paper products come from responsibly managed forests and recycled materials. The Programme for the Endorsement of Forest Certification (PEFC), on the other hand, certifies that paper products come from sustainably managed forests. Certifications relating to inks include the EU Ecolabel and the Nordic Swan, both of which encompass strict environmental and climate criteria.

3.7. Pushing the Boundaries of Innovation

Sustainable printing practices are continuously evolving, driven by innovative solutions like algae-based inks, stone paper, and electronic paper displays (EPDs). Incorporating these materials could not only minimize environmental harm but also revolutionize the feel and aesthetic of printed literature.

This may seem like a lot to take in, but taking steps towards sustainable printing is a journey. It won't happen overnight, and every little bit helps. The change is worthwhile. After all, each page we print less harmfully, is a step towards a more sustainable future.

Remember, as consumers, your choices also propel the industry forward. By choosing publishers that adhere to sustainable printing practices, you can contribute to the momentum needed to transform the industry. This is the power of sustainable printing. Every page you turn, you're committing to protect your planet.

Chapter 4. Sustainable Book Materials: Beyond Pulp and Ink

The landscape of sustainable literature is vast and intricate, intricately linked with our understanding of the environment. Central to this landscape is the concept of sustainable book materials, an area of focus which pushes the borders of traditional book manufacturing into territory that is both eco-friendly and ethically responsible.

4.1. Sustainable Paper: A New Dawn

The manufacturing of paper, traditionally, centers around wood from trees. However, sustainable literature is helping redefine this norm, introducing eco-friendly alternatives. Recycled paper is one such popular choice, consuming less energy, water, and producing fewer greenhouse gases relative to virgin paper.

According to the Environment Paper Network's Paper Calculator Version 4, using recycled paper, specifically post-consumer waste, results in 38-72% nett energy savings and 35% less water consumed compared to virgin fiber. It also diverts waste from landfills, closing the loop in the cycle of consumption and production.

But the Paper Calculator also highlights the complexity of the issue, showing that while recycled paper saves on energy, water use can vary depending on the de-inking process used. Moreover, different recycling processes can result in different levels of emissions, making it clear that the shift towards sustainability is an intricate one.

Besides recycling, tree-free alternatives like bamboo, hemp, and agricultural residues such as wheat straw and bagasse (sugar cane residue) are also promising sustainable sources. Bamboo, especially, holds promise, growing up to 20 times faster than trees and producing up to 20 times more fiber. Similarly, agricultural residues, often discarded or burnt after harvesting, can also be converted into paper.

4.2. Ink Evolution: From Petroleum to Soy

Ink is another major raw material in book manufacturing. Traditional inks, derived from petroleum, are rich in volatile organic compounds (VOCs) which are harmful to both the environment and human health.

In recent years, vegetable-based inks, primarily soy ink, have emerged as eco-friendly alternatives. Soy ink, made from soybeans, a renewable resource, is not just low on VOCs, but also provides more vibrant colors, making it an enticing proposition for publishers.

The American Soybean Association's SoySeal program helps identify products with soy ink. However, as soy ink doesn't completely eliminate VOCs, publishers should consider other factors like printing technology (such as waterless printing which reduces VOC emissions) and end-of-life management (like recycling or composting) when planning their sustainable printing strategy.

4.3. Going Beyond the Book: The Environmental Impact of Bindings and Covers

Sustainable book materials extend beyond just paper and ink. Other constituents of a book – the cover and the binding – must also be environmentally manageable.

Alternative materials such as recycled plastics, cork, and plant-based synthetics are being explored for covers. Despite the challenges such as durability and aesthetic appeal, these experiments with unconventional materials represent a significant step forward on the sustainability scale.

Binding materials have also evolved, featuring greater use of animal-free glue and stitching methods over plastic options. Like ink, the environmental impact of these materials isn't just about their production, but also how they decompose and are potentially recycled.

4.4. The Future Outlook: Innovation and Challenges

Discussions on sustainable book materials aren't complete without looking to the future. Innovations such as stone paper, made from limestone residues mixed with high-density polyethylene, and algae ink are proving that the possibilities are limitless.

While these innovations are promising, challenges remain. The higher costs of alternative materials and the lack of industry-wide standards are significant barriers. The availability of some materials, like bamboo, may also be a challenge due to other competing uses such as construction and textiles.

Nevertheless, even as we navigate these complexities, it is clear that the future of book materials is one that balances the magic of books with the need to protect our collective home. The road towards complete sustainability in literature is ongoing, and each stride taken along this journey reinforces the importance of consciously crafting our stories – not just within our books, but also through the materials we use to build them. The understanding of sustainable book materials is, indeed, an essential chapter in our larger narrative of sustainable living.

As we flip the pages of our sustainable books, we are also turning a new leaf in our story with the environment, one where each word we read and each page we turn is a testament to our commitment to harmony with nature. This balance is the essence of sustainable literature, a balance that we will continue to explore in the chapters to come.

Chapter 5. Authors Championing Environmental Stewardship

As we explore our roles in mitigating environmental degradation and advocating for sustainability, we cannot overlook the influential voices found in the literary realm. Authors, poets, journalists, and academics alike have used their platforms to highlight environmental issues and stewardship, fostering dialogues that encourage readers to reflect on their relationships with nature and our collective responsibility to the planet.

5.1. Building Green Narratives

Throughout history, a collection of authors has used the power of storytelling to urge serious contemplation of environmental protection. Their narratives built around ecology, nature, climate change, and resilience have not only increased readers' awareness but also influenced their attitudes towards environmental stewardship.

Rachel Carson, for example, was one of the early advocates for environmental conservation. Her seminal book, "Silent Spring," raised public awareness about the harmful effects of pesticides and triggered a nationwide conversation in the US about the nexus between ecological health and human welfare. Carson's rigorous scientific investigation combined with emotive prose was compelling, offering a new kind of environmental narrative that galvanized action.

Kenyan author, Ngũgĩ wa Thiong'o, in his book "The River Between," explores the conflict between tradition and modernity as it pertains to the land. His vivid storytelling creates a powerful reflection on the idea of respect for the natural world. His work demonstrates that acknowledging the importance of the land in keeping traditions alive is a form of environmental conservation itself.

5.2. Championing Environmental Causes in Literature

Many contemporary authors stand on the shoulders of these literary giants, cultivating environmental ideologies within their narratives. They address environmental challenges, propose sustainable solutions, and promote a more sophisticated understanding of the complex systems that govern our world and how we can better interact with it.

Currently, authors such as Margaret Atwood with her speculative fiction including "The Year of the Flood" and Richard Powers with his Pulitzer winning book "The Overstory" weave environmental themes into their narratives. They precipitate contemplation on our place in an increasingly threatened world, encouraging readers to become stewards of the environment.

5.3. Bridging the Gap: Academia into the Mainstream

A growing trend in the realm of environmental literature is the power of academic authors who bring complex science into accessible prose. They use their extensive knowledge to inform on important topics and to push society towards more sustainable behaviors.

Dr. Jane Goodall, a respected primatologist, anthropologist, and an excellent example of this group, enlightens readers about the significance of conserving wildlife, particularly chimpanzees, in her books like "Hope for Animals and Their World". Goodall's narrative brings to the forefront the relationship between humans and animals, emphasizing that the survival of both are intertwined.

Climate scientist, Dr. Katharine Hayhoe is another compelling author in this space. In her book "Saving Us: A Climate Scientist's Case for Hope and Healing in a Divided World," Hayhoe breaks down complex climate science and offers solutions that unite people rather than create division.

5.4. Children's Authors and Environmental Advocacy

Another group of authors driving environmental consciousness are those writing for children and young adults. Their works aim to instill stewardship principles and a love for nature early in life, thereby fostering responsible environmental behavior.

Dr. Seuss's "The Lorax," a classic among environmental children's literature, conveys a potent message about the harmful effects of industrialization on nature, reminding readers that, "Unless someone like you cares a whole awful lot, nothing is going to get better. It's not."

Lynne Cherry's "The Great Kapok Tree" tells of a man who falls asleep under the giant tropical tree he's supposed to chop down, only to be visited by its inhabiting animals and persuaded to let it stand. The book is an important read for young minds, teaching empathy for nature and the significance of preserving biodiversity.

5.5. Environmental Journalism: Writing for Change

Environmental journalism also plays a critical role in promoting planetary stewardship. Journalists and authors such as Naomi Klein,

Elizabeth Kolbert, and Bill McKibben have provided coverage of climate change, biodiversity loss, and environmental policy, aiming to inform, ignite action, and break the inertia in addressing our climatic reality.

Kolbert's Pulitzer-prize winning book, "The Sixth Extinction: An Unnatural History," investigates past extinctions and the ongoing biodiversity crisis. By making complicated scientific concepts accessible and relatable, this kind of investigative journalism can catalyze discussions on conservation, encourage critical thinking, and stimulate collective actions towards environmental stewardship.

5.6. Conclusion: A Call to Action

In our quest for environmental sustainability, words indeed hold great power. If harnessed strategically and convincingly as displayed by these environmental authors, the written word can be greened. Narratives, whether fictional or factual, have a unique ability to strike at the heart of audiences and incite change. This journey through the vast, green literary landscape reaffirms the power writers wield in creating a more environmentally-conscious world and revalidates the role of these champions of green literature in sculpting a hopeful future for our planet.

Chapter 6. Exploring Eco-conscious Genres and Themes in Literature

Understanding the environmental leaning in contemporary literature involves delving into different genres and themes. As diverse as our literary world is, so are the ways in which these eco-conscious elements manifest themselves - ranging from the use of nature as a context or the backdrop to directly addressing environmental issues in the storyline.

6.1. Poetry and the Environment

Poetry, due to the very nature of its form - concise, emotive, symbolic - has long been a mode of expression where writers explore their connections to, concerns for, and criticisms of the environment. Enriched by imageries of the natural world, environmental poetry often envelops readers with the beauty, mystery, and wisdom of nature.

The Romantic Poets - William Wordsworth, Samuel Taylor Coleridge, and John Keats - were notable voices echoing the wonders of the natural world during the late 18th and early 19th centuries. Their works imparted the poignant reminder of nature's enduring power and the havoc that human action could wreak on it.

Echoing these sentiments in the contemporary era, poets such as Mary Oliver and Wendell Berry have used their words to foreground the environmental ethos. Oliver's animal-eyed viewpoint places her amidst nature rather than above it. Similarly, Berry's farming poems deeply embody the ethos of sustainability and the necessity for mankind's harmony with nature.

6.2. Non-fiction Narratives: Memoirs and Reportage

Non-fiction narratives have proven to be impactful, directly addressing aspects such as climate change, deforestation, loss of biodiversity, and other pressing environmental problems. We find memoirs, personal narratives, investigative journalism, and academic texts deeply rooted in ecology.

Rachel Carson's 'Silent Spring' could be considered a seminal work in this genre, as it alerted the public to the harmful effects of pesticides on the environment. Other contemporary works like Elizabeth Kolbert's 'The Sixth Extinction' and Naomi Klein's 'This Changes Everything: Capitalism vs. the Climate' engage readers with the looming threat of climate change and the urgent need for sustainable solutions.

6.3. The Rise of Climate Fiction (Cli-Fi)

Nowadays, climate change has become a prevalent theme in fiction as well. The term 'Cli-Fi' has been coined to describe narratives that address the potential impacts of climate change on human societies.

These stories often mirror our anxieties about the future and speculate about the societal and personal impacts of an environment altered by human activity. Works like Barbara Kingsolver's 'Flight Behavior' and Paolo Bacigalupi's 'The Water Will Come' plunge directly into the effects of climate change and the human struggle to adapt.

6.4. Nature in Children's Literature

Children's literature has increasingly begun to echo the themes of environmental consciousness as educators and parents acknowledge the importance of early environmental education. Books like 'The Lorax' by Dr. Seuss, 'The Great Kapok Tree' by Lynne Cherry, or 'The Watcher' by Jeanette Winter convey environmental themes digestibly to young minds.

They beautifully encapsulate lessons on conservation, deforestation, and animal protection in understandable yet impactful narratives.

6.5. The Interplay of Science-Fiction and Ecology

Science-Fiction (Sci-Fi) has also embraced environmental themes, projecting the consequences of current environmental practices into future scenarios. Kim Stanley Robinson's Mars trilogy or Frank Herbert's 'Dune' series weave together geopolitics, environmentalism, and future societies, exploring how decisions today affect tomorrow.

Intriguingly, a sub-genre known as eco-punk emerged, highlighting themes of eco-sustainability in combined dystopian and utopian settings, pushing the boundaries of current thought on sustainability and human adaptation.

In conclusion, eco-conscious genres and themes are a growing part of our literary landscape, reflecting our increasing environmental awareness. From expressing our love and reverence for nature to critically engaging with our environmental footprints, literature, in its numerous genres, provides a profound and imaginative space to explore these issues. It not only educates but also invites readers to feel, question, and, importantly, act.

Chapter 7. Promoting Environmental Awareness through Children's Literature

Children's literature has always been a medium through which important values and ideas are taught. Over generations, stories and books have imparted lessons on morality, courage, resilience, and empathy. Today, as our planet faces some of the gravest environmental challenges, children's literature can play an instrumental role in fostering awareness about and respect for our environment. It provides a remarkable sphere of influence that can make children grasp the importance of caring for the environment from a young age.

7.1. The Importance of Environmental Education

Environmental education aims to nurture an understanding of how personal and social actions affect the natural world, promote appreciation for the environment, and foster informed actions to preserve it. Among the earliest forms of this education are children's books—works of literature that can spark interest and shape environmental attitudes.

Children's books have a potential for impacting profound environmental responsibility by integrating fun, imaginative stories with meaningful environmental themes. By talking about climate change, pollution, deforestation, or endangered species, these books enable children to understand the issues our planet faces and learn what they can do to help, even at their age. Also, by fostering a love for nature through books, children are more likely to grow into adults who respect and protect the environment.

7.2. The Role of Children's Books in Promoting Environmental Awareness

Children's books have a unique power to enlighten young minds about the importance of environmental preservation. They provide a platform where complex environmental issues can be simplified in an engaging manner, igniting curiosity and promoting an innate understanding of the environment.

These books often discuss environmental issues subtly through the journey of the characters, helping children build a strong emotional connection with the message. Often, stories depict characters who take steps to protect the environment, encouraging young readers to emulate these behaviors. For example, a book about a young girl who plants trees in her town not only teaches children about the benefits of trees but also encourages them to take similar steps in their communities.

7.3. The Impact of Illustrated Books on Environmental Education

Illustrated books, in particular, can have a lasting impact on children's understanding of environmental duties. The vivid and colorful depictions of flora, fauna, and landscapes can foster a love for nature from a young age. Illustrations serve as visual aids to the written content and often portray the beauty of nature and its creatures, either in their raw form or anthropomorphized, which makes the stories both relatable and engaging.

These illustrations can also effectively convey the consequences of harmful human behaviors towards the environment. For instance, pictures showing the devastation caused by deforestation or pollution provide an impactful visual learning experience. They manage to capture the stark reality of environmental damage, making it tangible for young readers.

7.4. Lessons from Prominent Children's Books about the Environment

Several children's literature pieces have tackled crucial environmental issues, each in its unique style. For example, "The Lorax" by Dr. Seuss, one of the most renowned children's books with an environmental message, teaches about the devastating impacts of industrialization on nature. Through engaging rhymes and captivating illustrations, it instills a powerful message of responsible consumption and caretaking of the environment.

Another classic, "The Great Kapok Tree" by Lynne Cherry, tells the tale of a man who, intending to cut down a massive rainforest tree, falls asleep only to be visited by the jungle's inhabitants pleading for the tree's life. This story teaches children about the interdependent nature of ecosystems and the importance of preserving them.

Newer works like "The Watcher" by Jeanette Winter introduces children to the pioneering conservationist Jane Goodall and her work with chimpanzees, reinforcing respect for all living creatures and weaving a narrative around the need for environmental and animal conservation.

In each of these instances, the books leave a lasting impression, fostering a sense of environmental stewardship among young readers. The messages they convey vary, encompassing wide-ranging themes like conservation, ethos of care, biodiversity, sustainable behaviors, and the potential impacts of environmental degradation.

7.5. Inculcating Sustainable Practices through Children's Books

Beyond educating children about environmental issues, children's literature can provide them with actionable steps to start their journey as environmental stewards. Stories can incorporate elements encouraging children to adopt sustainable practices, like recycling, planting trees, reducing water use, and so on.

For example, a story where the characters practice sorting waste into recyclables and compost can instill in children an understanding of waste management. Likewise, a tale revolving around a neighborhood clean-up can motivate them to participate in similar community services. It's about reinforcing the idea that "every little helps," and even small actions can make a big difference.

7.6. Closing Thoughts

Cultivating environmental awareness in young minds is a critical step towards ensuring a sustainable future. Through engaging narratives, memorable characters, and convincingly woven environmental messages, children's books play a fundamental role in this endeavor. As such, they hold the power to shape the environmental consciousness of the next generation, and as custodians of the planet, it is our responsibility to make the most of such influential tools. At the intersection of children's literature and environmental awareness lies the potential to create a future generation that values and fights for the survival and sustenance of our planet.

Let's promote and appreciate the authors and illustrators who are contributing to this crucial literary space. Remember, the seeds we sow in youthful minds today can grow into a forest of environmental stewards tomorrow.

Chapter 8. Eco-friendly Bookstores and Libraries around the World

Therein lies the increasing recognition that creating enjoyable reading habits must not come at the expense of our planet. Physical locations like bookstores and libraries play an essential role in promoting sustainable practices in literature. These green spaces have become global phenomena and are taking initiatives aimed at positively impacting our Earth.

8.1. Eco-Friendly Bookstores

Eco-friendly bookstores are changing the face of retail, demonstrating that bookselling can be environmentally conscious. One such example is the amazing P.S. Bookshop in Brooklyn, New York. This bookstore sells a variety of used and rare books, ensuring each of them gets a second life while reducing waste from new book manufacturing processes. To further its environmental efforts, P.S. Bookshop uses energy-efficient lighting and has a strict recycling program in place.

Over the ocean, you will find the famous Bókin Bookstore in Reykjavik, Iceland. This unique store, with its endless sprawl of used books, showcases how much potential exists for achieving sustainability through secondhand sales. Bókin Bookstore strives to give each book a new home, in turn helping to conserve natural resources.

Then we have Better World Books, a worldwide online bookstore that champions sustainability at its core. They not only sell used books, reducing waste and encouraging reuse, but also commit to matching each purchase with a book donation to someone in need.

Furthermore, for every book that cannot be sold or donated, Better World Books ensures that it's recycled, thus avoiding unnecessary landfill contribution.

8.2. Libraries Pioneering in Environmental Sustainability

Libraries have traditionally been havens for readers, offering free access to a trove of knowledge. However, in recent years, many have also stepped up to the plate in terms of ecological responsibility. They are creating green spaces that promote environmental awareness while remaining committed to their traditional roles.

Denver Public Library in Colorado, USA, was the winner of the U.S. Green Building Council's 2003 Leadership in Energy and Environmental Design (LEED) award. The library's newest branches are built incorporating energy-efficient technologies that utilize natural light, reducing electricity use. Native plants that require less water and care surround the buildings, and recharge stations for electronic vehicles are available for patrons.

Across the globe in Singapore, we find the National Library building, which received the first Green Mark Platinum Award from the Building and Construction Authority (BCA) in 2005. The building is designed to maximize the use of natural light and ventilation, and it harnesses solar energy to power certain parts of the facility. In keeping with the tropical environment, the exterior "lends a hand" by having unique sunshades and even a lush sky garden, to help in reducing the urban heat island effect.

In Australia, the Oran Park Library took green building several steps further by incorporating design elements that are intended to educate visitors about sustainability. The building includes displays that show real-time electricity and water usage, roof gardens for growing fresh produce, and a recycling system for rainwater.

8.3. Sustainable Reading Rooms

These reading rooms are part of eco-conscious libraries and are a silence-filled testament to the commitment toward a greener future. Helsinki's Oodi library in Finland, known for its stunning architecture, fosters natural light in the building, reducing the need for artificial illumination. Its book-sorting robot not only stirs interest but also conserves energy compared to traditional systems.

In the UK, The Hive in Worcester is an iconic gold-clad building with vast solar panels capturing a significant portion of its electricity needs. The structure includes a built-in rainwater harvesting system, optimizing water utility.

8.4. The Future of Eco-Literate Retail

This movement will continue to gather momentum in bookselling and library sectors as they optimize their operations for sustainability. Improved waste management practices, water-efficient systems, solar energy installations, and innovative architecture that harnesses natural lighting and ventilation are just some strategies being pursued.

Emerging technologies such as e-ink displays and virtual reality could also be harnessed to enhance the environmental friendliness of bookstores and libraries. In a world grappling with the urgent need to reduce carbon emissions, organizations promoting literacy need to ensure they are also promoting stewardship of the Earth. It's not merely a trend – it's an imperative.

In summary, eco-friendly bookstores and libraries around the world have taken initiatives to ensure their practices reduce harm to the environment. They are creatively repurposing and recycling books, using energy and water efficiently, and utilizing green construction principles. These steps promote not only a love for literature but also a respect for our planet, making us all part of the solution to the multifaceted challenges of sustainability. As these green initiatives gain traction, they continue to influence and reshape the way we think about sustainable literacy in the 21st century.

Chapter 9. Digital Literature: An Eco-friendly Alternative?

As advancements in technology continue to reshape our everyday lives, the impact on the traditional publishing industry is undeniable. Moving away from paper, many authors, publishers, and readers are transitioning towards digital literature, an increasingly popular means of consuming literature that provides a viable alternative to physical books. Digital literature not only offers modern convenience and versatile formatting but also brings to the fore a key advantage - environmental sustainability.

9.1. The Evolution of Digital Literature

Digital literature refers to works of literature conveyed through digital mediums like e-books, online articles, blogs, digital comics, and so forth. This form of literature surfaced with the rise of the digital age, starting in the late 20th century when the Internet started reaching millions worldwide. Early instances of digital literature were limited to electronic versions of physical books. Today, digital literature encompasses much more, from interactive e-books with sound effects and animations to hypertext narratives which allow for non-linear reading experiences.

9.2. Going Green with Digital Reading

While printed books possess a romantic charm and tangible quality that many readers cherish, the production process involved often leads to significant environmental damage. Harvesting of trees for paper contributes to deforestation, while factories making ink and book-binding materials emit harmful pollutants. On the contrary, digital literature cuts down these environmental costs drastically.

An electronic book, once published online, can be downloaded and read by countless individuals, sans the paper, ink, or physical transport expense. This significantly reduces greenhouse gas emissions, helping in the fight against climate change. Thus, digital literature is an eco-friendly alternative that allows educators, authors, readers to contribute to environmental conservation efforts while still engaging with the literary world.

9.3. The Aligning Technology and Environment

Various technologies fuel digital literature, and it's important to note that these technologies have environmental impacts as well. Devices for reading e-books, such as Kindles, tablets, smartphones, and computers, all require significant amounts of energy to produce and operate.

However, with increasing movements towards green technologies, strides have been made to improve the efficiency of these devices to last longer and use less energy. Solar-powered e-readers and energy-efficient tablets provide greener alternatives for avid readers. Digital libraries hold the potential to host vast amounts of literature without the spatial constraints and environmental footprint of physical libraries.

9.4. The Accessibility and Versatility of Digital Literature

Digital literature is not just environmentally friendly; it's remarkably accessible too. Digital books can be accessed instantly from anywhere around the globe, reducing the need for physical distribution networks and contributing further to reduced carbon emissions. This democratizes access to a wide array of literature, often including free, open-source materials.

Furthermore, the versatility of digital literature leads to new combinations of text, graphics, sound, and interaction, offering unique experiences for educators, authors, and readers alike. This can also contribute to improving literacy skills by engaging different types of learners.

9.5. Digital Literature – The Way Forward

Ultimately, the move towards digital literature promises a greener publishing future. As readers, we can choose to align with this shift, understanding that our love for the written word doesn't have to contribute to environmental degradation.

While nothing can replace the feel of a book, the rise of digital literature presents a timely opportunity to bring our reading habits in line with the increasing need for sustainability. By doing so, we can honour our planet while still immersing ourselves in the magic of words. Visions of the future library may include more pixels than paper, but if it leads to a healthier planet, it might just be a future worth reading towards.

In conclusion, the promise of digital literature and its eco-friendly potential offers an exciting avenue for book-lovers to explore. It's another reminder of how our actions, even those as simple as choosing to download an e-book, can help write the story of a greener, more sustainable future. As we turn the digital pages of this chapter, we acknowledge that with every shared word, there is a responsibility and an opportunity to affect change. Through embracing digital literature, we can play a part in ensuring a more literary, and sustainable, world to come.

Chapter 10. The Role of Readers in Promoting Sustainable Literature

Our engagement with literature is a deeply intimate journey, often seen as solitary. Yet, when readers come together, they wield immense power to drive change, including fostering sustainability in literature. The key to effective readership lies in education, awareness, and action steps toward sustainable reading. This chapter outlines the role of readers in propelling a greener future for literature.

10.1. Transparency and Ethical Consumerism

Readers can influence sustainability in literature by supporting transparency and ethical consumerism. Predominantly, consumers' awareness of sustainability issues has led many industries to adopt eco-friendly practices. Hence, when readers demand transparency about the environmental footprint of their books, publishers will increasingly provide this information, fostering a more holistic accountability ecosystem.

You can start this journey by buying books printed on FSC-certified paper, supporting publishers that use eco-friendly inks, or choosing books bound in sustainable materials. Ask your local library or bookstore about their sustainability efforts, and if those aren't satisfactory, express your concern. Put simply; use your buying power to reinforce sustainability.

10.2. Embrace Digital Reading

While a physical book provides a sensory experience electronic books can't match, e-reading is a potent tool towards sustainability. By choosing digital books and magazines, you can significantly lighten your environmental footprint.

Consider these figures:

- A mid-range e-reader, used regularly over five years, has a lighter carbon footprint than printing a handful of niche physical books.

- Powering an e-reader for an hour results in a carbon footprint equivalent to printing 0.007 paperback books.

- If an e-reader replaces 50 paperbacks, the carbon footprint is reduced by 70%.

Certainly, digital reading isn't perfect — the energy for device production, charging, and internet use must be considered — but if used judiciously, it can make a big difference.

10.3. Participating in Book Sharing and Second-Hand Platforms

One of the most sustainable ways to read is by sharing books. Before buying new, see if you can borrow the book from a library or a friend, or buy it second-hand. This not only reduces the environmental impact of producing new books, but it also prolongs the life of existing ones.

Book swaps, also known as book exchanges, are a fantastic way to rejuvenate your book collection without contributing to unnecessary consumption or waste. Various websites and apps facilitate book swapping, not to mention local swap fairs or library programs.

10.4. Reading and Promoting Eco-themed Literature

Promoting books with eco-themes, such as climate change, conservation, and sustainable living is another proactive step for readers. When we read and discuss these topics, we increase our own understanding and raise awareness in our communities.

This is particularly influential for younger readers, as incorporating environmental issues in children's literature can sow seeds of knowledge, empathy, and action concerning the natural world.

10.5. Personal Sustainability Actions

We can further promote sustainability in our reading habits by implementing personal actions. These may range from using energy-efficient reading lamps or blackout curtains that maximize natural light, to reusing or upcycling older books, or recycling books that can no longer be used.

In essence, the reader's role in promoting sustainable literature is expansive and proactive. By focusing on ethical consumerism, embracing digital reading, fostering a culture of sharing and exchange, promoting eco-themed literature, and committing to personal acts of sustainability, we aren't merely passive consumers. Instead, we become active participants in the creation of a more sustainable literary landscape, paying homage to the very essence of literature itself: a tool for understanding, change, and celebration of our shared human experience on this beautiful planet.

Chapter 11. The Future of Green Literature: Trends and Predictions

In the bustling realm of publications and manuscripts, a verdant revolution is taking place as we stride optimistically towards a future of sustainable literature. This chapter focuses on the anticipated trends and predictions in green literature, penned down to enlighten our readers on how the literary world is advancing while maintaining its eco-consciousness.

11.1. Technological Innovations in Publishing

In the modern age, technology and innovation have seeped into every aspect of our lives, publishing not being an exception. From typewriters to computers, and now to cloud-based platforms, technology has always been a dependable ally of publishing. In the future, we can expect to see these technological innovations metamorphose to a more sustainable platform.

Emerging technologies like blockchain, known for its powers in the finance world, are expected to revolutionize publishing, allowing greater transparency and security. Blockchain could transfer rights and royalties directly to authors, reducing waste generated by traditional, complex publishing processes.

The era of AI and Machine Learning will bring about enhanced analytics that can help publishers better understand their readers, tailor content to their preferences, and thereby potentially reduce unwanted print runs. In addition, AI can also step in as the new-age editor, highlighting areas for improvements – a future that replaces ink and paper edits with digital suggestions.

The burgeoning trend of print-on-demand models too suggests a future where waste is minimized. Books will no longer be printed in surplus, reducing both paper waste and costs associated with storage.

11.2. The Advent of Sustainable Materials

Sustainability has become a significant parameter in the choice of materials used in publishing. Looking ahead, we can expect this trend to become more predominant, with traditional printing materials gradually being replaced by eco-friendly alternatives.

In the realms of paper production, we are likely to see widespread adoption of environmentally friendly practices. This will include the use of recycled paper, tree-free paper made from crops like hemp or bamboo, and paper processed without chlorine.

Even inks used for printing are evolving, with more publishers favoring vegetable-based over petroleum-based inks due to their lower VOC emissions and easier de-inking during the recycling process.

Advancements in book cover materials must also be acknowledged. Eco-friendly alternatives such as Bio-laminates, made from biodegradable cellulose film, will likely become a common sight.

11.3. Digitalization and E-books

The adoption and acceptance of E-books has surged in the past decade with advancements in digital technology, and this trend shows no sign of slowing down. As digital natives become a larger part of the reading demographic, this transition to digital platforms will further gain momentum.

The emergence of feature-rich reading platforms and devices with adjustable font, low-light reading modes, and integrated dictionaries will continue to make E-books a palatable solution for conscientious readers.

However, it's not just the characteristics of these digital platforms that are appealing. The reduced carbon footprint associated with the creation and distribution of E-books in contrast with their printed counterparts suggests a bright future for this digital transition.

11.4. Authors and Environmental Advocacy

Authors wield a tremendous power in advocating for environmental sustainability. The future of green literature would be incomplete without discussing this influential cadre. Upcoming authors are more inclined towards environmental advocacy and that is mirrored in their literary works. Climate change fiction, or cli-fi, is a fast-growing genre that weaves environmental concerns and predictions into engaging narratives to raise awareness regarding our planet's health.

These trends, however, are not confined only to a particular genre. The themes of environmental conservation, sustainable living, and rekindling our connection with nature are expected to permeate across different genres, from mystery to romance and science fiction.

11.5. Environmental Education and Literature

Another trend in green literature is educational. An increasing number of works will be designed to engage students of all ages in understanding and appreciating our fragile environment. These might be in the form of textbooks, graphic novels, or children's books bearing engaging visuals and easy-to-understand content, aimed at making complex environmental concepts comprehensible to the young minds.

The future beckons for more literature to incorporate sustainability in its core narrative or serve as a strategy of fostering environmental stewardship.

We hope this journey into the future of Green Literature has piqued your interest and heightened awareness. It does not merely hint at the pivotal role that literature will play in the coming decades, it also serves to remind us that every action counts towards shaping a sustainable future. The green revolution, it appears, is not confined to the fields. It also flourishes in the pages of the books we lovingly hold.

www.ingramcontent.com/pod-product-compliance
Lightning Source LLC
LaVergne TN
LVHW051632050326
832903LV00033B/4726